FLIGHTLESS BIRD- BLUE

A POETRY BOOK

SHREEJOYEE

Made with ❤ on the Notion Press Platform
www.notionpress.com

Contents

Contents

Prologue

Flightless bird, can we fly ever again? These walls never let us breathe but whenever we let them down, we end up bleeding.

Is this a flight or a free fall?

1. Brighter than the stars

You are like the cold breeze on a hot day .
You are like the rain which soothes the heated ground .
You are the sparkling star which makes the night view more beautiful .
You are the mid view of day and night .
You are like the wandering clouds ,
The clouds which portraits the sky with illusional images .
My love is like counting the stars at night .
You are the tree shade on an exhausting day .
You are like the spider , making cobwebs in my heart .
You are the earthy smell when rain hits the ground .
You are just like the sky , which always flaunt in pretty colours .

2. World's Prejudice

I hope that the walls disappear soon
and soon we could walk under the sunshine
with no measures in front of the world
i hope the day arrives soon
i hope that the world captures our beauty
with no discrimination
we'd hold our hand and step together
no matter what happens
the sunlight would be so bright with anti discrimination
i hope the day comes when we'd fight back together having
eachother's side
darling , you know
how the world is cruel
but i promise to protect you
and hold you
until the end
until the last breath
i would seize you within me
i'd hold you as the most precious thing in the universe
there's is no second of you and will never be
as you're my one and only
i hope the day arrives soon

when there would be no partition
when it will be just Us in the world
portraying our love infront of the world
i hope the day arrives soon !

3. Scarlet my heart- touch it, golden

You know what is my greatest poetry ?
not the one which i write about you
or the poem which is about you
because all my poems bows infront of your eyes .
you yourself is a fine art ,
a poetry , a magic ,
which I engrave in paper and tombstone
to make something like you ,
to make something as exquisite as us .
but can never compete the original
and neither do I want .
You are the most beautiful form of Stardust.
You've curled myself within you ,
like the sea engulfs the shore .
And your invisible form of poetry made me a poet .
Invisible against the world .
You are the treasure with mysteries -
the more i unfold ,
the more i solve .
The more i fall for those eyes .

And the treasure which i want to discover each new day ,
is YOU ,
My Greatest Poetry .
My Sunlight ,
we'd survive this Great War
hold my hands , my Love .
we can Smile .

4. Tristful

Do you know how special the stars are ?
It shines and glimmers in the dark
even if the world is the darkness ,
it still give Hopes .
The stars are the beauty of the sky
without which it loses its beauty .
The stars are millions of miles away
still gives glimpses to us .
It is even destroyed
but it's effect doesn't go away
giving it's reflection .
Just like the Stars and Moon
are lovers Forever ,
Be my Lover Forever .
Just like the stars and moon
go through sad and happy phases together ,
let's go together too !
Just like the stars and moon hold eachother ,
Be my star and i shall be your moon
holding eachother Forever .

5. Dull Love

What if the moon and night have conversations among themselves?
what if the moon gets angry with the night
what if it says to the night not to come so fast
as the moon has to get separated from the stars
from their love
and has to talk and see from distance
what if the moon weeps for the stars
to be always with her
and not to visit the earth
But , what if the night has ' something ' for moon
what if the night comes fast just to visit moon
what if the night comes fast just to glare at the moon
what if the dark night has something bright within ?
what if the dark night has stories to share with the moon
and wants to be with the moon
but all it does is to stay numb
what if the night cries in the light for the moon
what if the night loves the moon and the moon loves the stars ?
what if the night remains dark only for the moon to shine bright
what if the night comes to sing for the moon
what if the night comes everyday to say the three magical words

to the moon
what if the night has said the three magical words
but is waiting for years
for the love
what if the night denies love after non acceptance
but loves from distant
what if it still cries
what if the night is still hoping for acceptance
what if the love triangle stays forever
what if the night always has to stay broken
what if the night stays dark only to adore the moon from distance
even if the moon's chemistry is with the stars
maybe the secret of night's darkness is only for the moon
maybe the moon can never see the dull night's love as it's bright
and it chooses what glimmers
what if the moon's realisation is too late
when the world ends
and the love triangle ends too.

6. Tough times are like battles

You don't know how I feel
when you ask me to leave you ,
when you ask me to hang up the call ,
when you say " i don't wanna talk about this " ,
you don't know how it feels .
How the words poke my heart
and gives a pinning pain ,
whenever you leave with grudges .
It feels like you are gone
leaving me behind .
It feels like you don't wanna argue
just because you are bored .
Oh darling ,
I don't know how to explain this
but i want to be there for you ,
in your both up's and downs !
I don't wanna leave you in your worst .
I want to know every inch of you ,
in every way possible ,
even in your defeat .

I don't know if it sounds clingy
but i wanna stay with you
even in the moments when you want to fight alone ,
I wanna fight with you together .
I wanna be with you together .
cause all i have is you ,
and leaving you behind
in the battle ,
pierces my soul .
Ik you ask me to leave you
so that i don't get hurt
but baby ,
leaving you alone
hurts me the most .
I will never mind to get bruised in the battle
rather i would be happy to be your companion
and we fought together .
O beloved ,
let's fight together
and be eachother's strength
and never leave eachother behind
even in our sturdy times .

7. Stars and ends with you

My world ,
you lie at the bottom of my heart
living in a beautiful garden of flowers .
I breathe in the scent of the flowers
which is the same as yours .
i never searched for you
yet you came coincidentally in my life ,
in my world ,
where you own the place
where my world is in your name .
I treasure my world with you .
I treasure everything related to you .
the world seems so dark ,
so hazy ,
except the world which we created .
I founded the most shining star in the galaxy
which always glimmers
and stays with the moon .
darling , you're my North Star
and I'm your moon .
I hope you know
how my world starts with your name and ends with yours !

8. Golden Story

They don't know our story
they don't know how it is feels to be in love
there can be clouds crawling in the sky
but the rainbow proves that
after effect can be a bliss
you are the art which is so hard to define
but a pleasure to feel
you are always in my mind
I can't stop loving you
I can't take my eyes off you
Every little thing which you do is magic
you are my lucky star
I think this is the crazy little thing which people call as love
you are the crazy love
you are my girl
you are my love
my endless love
I am lost in love
baby , have I told you lately
that I shall keep on loving you
and hold your hand till the end
and I shall always be grateful that somehow we ended up

together
that somehow , in this infinite universe , we found eachother
and I shall always be grateful for that

9. It's always home with you

You know which are the hardest days ?
The days when we ignore eachother ,
the days when we overthink and communicate less .
The days when we cry for eachother ,
the days when we feel "it will not last long" .
The days seem to be even tougher -
when we don't show affection
and weep on eachother
but still choose to be silent .
Isn't the days unpleasant?
When we try to act as if we don't care
but we do !
Sometimes the way ,
the days pass by is like a night terror ,
haunting my reality .
It doesn't seem to end
I wake up screaming for you ,
tears free falling my eyes ,
then I find myself back in your arms .
At home , I feel again ,

inhaling your scent .

10. Fragile Feather

Sometimes in a relationship ,
we fly so high
and it's pretty satisfying anh exhilarating .
But the fall from the high ,
hurts so bad !
It breaks our bones
and tears us apart .
It makes us realise the height .
The bruises and scars become so deep
that it's hard to heal .
The hurt is within ,
It pains so badly .
It has no more noises or screams !
It is deep within .
It shivers , it pains ,
It's so hard to bear ,
but still it stays .
It has so much to say
but it chooses silence .
If people knew the future ,
that conquering the sky would cost so much ,
they would never fly .

They'd shed their feathers off ,
they'd cut their feathers off
and cherish the flow of blood .
They'd be in so much peace to self hurt
rather to fall .
It hurts to see the height from the ground ,
after falling ,
where we once were flying ,
where we once were cherishing the blue sky and sunlight .
But now it seems so dark ,
It seems so cloudy with full of haze .
Why do we fall directly ?
Why aren't their stairs ?
Because it hurts so bad after falling !

Chapter11

It's not an illicit affair

We will be open

So pretend.

12. Love you like I'm losing you

I was dreaming of roses and daisies
In a moonlit night
We were walking hand in hand
You pulled me closer
Kissed my hand
In split of a second you were not there
I was left alone.
I was shaking like a leaf on a stormy night
I woke up crying and screaming
I looked beside me
And saw you asleep.
The relief that flooded through my veins
I touched your cheeks
Your warmth spread throughout my body
I pulled you closer
And held you so tight
That if you have to leave
You'd have to take me along with you.

I realised
We're not promised tomorrow
Our string can break
The world can end
So I decided to have no regrets.
I will love you like this is the last day
I will love you like there is no tomorrow
I will give all my love to you today
And if we're together tomorrow
Then I will do it all over again.
Today I'll love you like I'm losing you
I'll say the goodbye like it's the last one
What we have, I won't take it for granted
I'll kiss you a little bit longer
Because tomorrow we might not be here.
I'll whisper all my love to you
All the poems and songs that I wrote about you
I'll whisper it all to you
Before we run out of time
We can't help it if the smoke is in our eyes
So I'll love you like it's the last time.
I will not wait for any special day to say, "i love you"
I will tell that to you today
There's no need for waiting for special days
Your love lights up the entire town
So I'll tell you that I'm in love
Kiss you a little bit longer.

No, were not promised forever
I'll try to keep this fire alive
But we might run out of time
So I'll give all my love to you today
And if we get a tomorrow I'll do you over again.

13. Heal just to maim

We were playing fight
I didn't know you were actually into it
I handed you a knife just to get the vibe
You stabbed it into my heart.
The blood that spurt out of the wound
You said it's just water
I gave you knife with the trust of my heart
Why did you stab it into my heart?
Why did you have to do this?
What was shinny, now it's all rusted
Why did you have to do this?
You punched me in the place I'm the weakest
Now I can't breathe.
I'd run out of the scarlet in my veins
Why did you have to do this?
What was somehow fixed,
Now it's broken and worse
How my skin iches just to feel my emotions ooze out
Why did you have to do this?
Broke the promise with which I trusted you the most.
How you removed my brown tinge
And made me shine

Now I'm rusted.
Why did you have to be treacherous to the kingdom in glory?
Now the king's dead.

14. Relentless zeal-you touch my heart

Hold onto me
Like the ocean holds onto the shore
Coming back to it each everytime
Even after the hailstorms
It submerges the sand
Like it's the owner of the land
Just like you're the owner of my heart.
Kiss my lips
Like the rain kisses the thirsty land
The land savouring the drops to quench it's thirst
Like you extinguish the burn in my heart
With just the touch of your lips.

Pull me close
So that I can hide my face
On the crooke of your neck
Like we hide OURSELVES from the world
Kiss my forehead
And say, "we'd survive"
And I'd close my eyes

Just to believe it.
If you look deep into my eyes
Probably you can see
How it glistens for you
Probably you can see
How my heart skips a beat
Whenever you touch my hand
Probably you'd see
How I'm the happiest whenever I'm with you
Probably you'd understand
The underlying meanings of my poems
Probably you'd understand
How my heart yearns to feel your touch.
All these sonnets
Makes me a poet
Your love
Wants me to romanticise
How the sunset looks from my window
The wave of current that flows through my heart
When you smile at me
I always go back to you
And I love the way
You caress my cheeks on my lonely nights.
Lap me with your water
Engulf me within yourself
This love is relentless
I'd give all my might to you

I trust your words
I'd survive
Till you keep this fire alive
I'd curl into you
When your waves hit my shore.

15. Scarlet tattoo over my heart

Probably I didn't understand what you meant by forever
It was until you got over
My heart wasn't ready to feel the stab
My voice shook at the bridge of the song that I wrote for you
It was black all around.
They say get over
But they don't see it
When my bones break white
They don't see when my blood turns purple
They don't feel it
When the broken ribs pierce into my heart.
Probably I didn't understand the language that you spoke
I didn't know you use it for everyone you meet
"Forever" was carved in my heart with a dagger.
If I could leave this town
Then I'd do it right now
If I could crawl up from where I came
Then I'd do it right now
But before leaving
I'd write you a letter

Romance scribbled in cursive and slanting and shining letters.
I heard your stories
I was a devotee
When I saw her fix your shirt
A spark of jealousy
And lump in my throat
I didn't know it was possible to feel so much all together.
I wasn't ready to feel your hatred
The uncanny way you behaved with me
Didn't warn me enough
Nothing can warm the cold hailstorm in my heart
Probably I didn't know we'd have the shortest forever
The language that you taught me to speak
I'm dumb
The fire that you ignited
Burned my whole town down.
When they say looks can kill
They really does
The way you look at me
Kills me a thousand times
Every single day
My trepidation
Makes me nauseous
Probably I didn't understand
Forever was just two years for you
Then you got over.

Your name tattooed over my heart
Right where you'd always belong.

16. Dazed Oblivion

The 31st
Each time I think about it
Takes me back to the winter'19
When we kissed for the last time.
If I'm the moth
You're the flame
I fly into you
It burns me
And taints my skin
But the way you're so luring
I fly back to you
Each time to die.
The wounds in my body
Burns
And stings
And bleeds
But I keep doing it
Because it helps me breathe.
The signs were in front of my eyes
I made them unseen
This love was not just amorous
The cradle to my grave.

When they take their lives
People say, "how selfish!"
But
Do you know
How many times she went half ways through it
Returned because of you
How many nights she scream for help
How many days she just wishes to be invisible
How you make it a bit more tough
You don't understand
How she asks the moon to heal her soul
The excruciating feeling from the lack of breath
And she hides her scars from you
Because they make her feel alive.
She sleeps because
It's her escapism
It's hard to cope when you can't breathe
Your ignorance
Makes it worse
Her sweetheart broke her trust and heart
How do I keep going!
The flame burnt in my heart
I gave my life as the fuel
I exist
They see me
But I have died the day
You threw me off the cliff.

When the clock will strike midnight
Probably I won't exist anymore
When the whole world will celebrate the New Year
I'd become invisible in the dazzled sky
The moon will open her arms for me
Will take me in her embrace
Sing me a lullaby
I'd sleep in peace
I don't want to be anywhere, where you're not with me.

17. Chérie, princesse

Darling, did you know how crazy it was
On the summer nights
When we used to walk for hour
When the sky used to be so bright and full of glimmering stars
When the breeze blew on your face.
Darling, did you know
When I looked into your eyes
It was as if the rest of my world disappeared
'Cause I was looking at my entire world
My sun and earth and moon
The exquisite paining ever created
My ecstasy
My bliss.
Lover, the summer evenings when we used to walk hand in hand
The exhilaration rushed through my veins
My soul fluttered a bit more whenever you smiled
My heart was captivated.
My love,
The love we had
Was different from the rest of the world
You were my bestfriend
But I was in love.

Don't know about you
But the sun and the moon knows
You were real to me
My sweetheart
This heart,
It burns
And pines
And perishes
Just for you.
We keep repeating
To be left stranded in an empty space
Your heart
"Fool you're back at it again."

18. Hopelessly devoted to you, beloved

Peerless
My heart was casketed just to be unlocked by you
You settled on the core of it
Built a fire place
To keep yourself warm
And I was warm too.
You'd hold my hand
And say," I love you the most"
I thought you meant it
My heart would burst with happiness.
The day we started
I knew what I was getting myself into
But your heart seemed so enticing
I wanted to make my way to it.
You were pressed on the wall
Our lips were dancing together
While my heart was intertwining with yours
I opened the blinds
And let you into it without another thought.

You pushed me off
Left my hand
The Christmas lights weren't bright enough to light up my heart
The Christmas hallelujahs weren't strong enough to hold us together
The penitence wasn't good enough
You left my hand
And heart and soul.
You didn't kiss me goodbye
You just walked away
Let the thunder
The avalanches
Make their way to my soul
From the missing pieces you took with yourself.
But I don't repent
Making you my sun
My sunshine
My felicity
My euphoria
I don't repent falling for you.
'Cause in this lifetime
Atleast I know how love burns your heart so passionately
I know how consuming it is
And I pity people who don't know how it feels to be this in love.
In this lifetime
Or another lifetime
I'd never think of love

Without thinking of you
But if someone ever asks you who your best lover was
I want you to think of me
'Cause you were the moon to my night sky
You were the scarlet in my veins
You were the last dream of my soul
And if you look deep into my eyes
Probably you can see the truth behind the clouds.
So, let me write the saddest poems of all time
How I loved you
And sometimes probably you had loved me too
In the night sky
Full of glimmering stars
I search for your eyes
Because none of them shine like the two stars you own
And this might be the last poem I write
Because any day without you
Seems like a bridge between dream and reality
And this might be my closure
Because this heart is nothing without you
These eyes have run out of tears
So, let me wish you
Goodnight, sweetheart
My heart will always remember you
Even when I'm not around
Just remember
I was you best lover

My, sweetest sweetheart.
Before this slumber
Can I get a touch of your lips
For the last time?
My sun
I'd take it with me
You and I against the world
My, beloved
My, lover.

19. Felicity-my daylight

My heart was golden for you
You painted my sky violet
My skin was glimmering with the golden glitters
Now I try to hide the marks you left.
We said we were compassionate
Did your words not mean anything?
You don't even have penitence
My body has marks from the lack of your love.
I was falling deep into the ocean of your love
They say, "love feels like flying"
But it's the semblance
How you made it look like
I didn't realise I was drowning
This love didn't keep me afloat
Felt it when I heard my bones break
No one heard my heart break
Lover, what did you do!
I drown into the grief
No ship is there to rescue me out
Sinking so deep that the sunlight can't reach me anymore
Just the memories of US all around
I can't breathe.

My world spins when I see you
The sick feeling crawls up my throat
As if someone is chocking me
I can't breathe anymore
Help me breathe.
The marks are there fresh and alive
No one can see the burnt bruises on my heart
I cry out for help
But no one can hear
Till I speak out loud
They say, "it's the demon in your mind, fight it. No one can help"
"I can't do this anymore"
And I'm overeating
It's just because I think too much about YOU.
I claw on people's hands to help me shake alive
They can't see me
They can't hear me
My muffled cries
The marks I make
A few tear drops I shed
I sign
To keep it in
They can't hear me cry
They can't see my heart breaking agonizingly.
Never searched for the bliss
But found the ecstasy in you
A single tear drop rolls down my eyes

I scream
But they can't hear
My felicity, I lost you.

20. Menace

I'm not afraid of the dark
The monsters they creep out from behind the bushes
As the clock stricks midnight thier sinister laugh
And their eerie footsteps on my threshold.
The monsters outside my door are merely haunting
The eyes which looked like the twinkling stars
Now when I look into them are cold
I see the demons in your eyes
Hiding behind your smile.
The juxtaposition of your semblance and real self
Puts me in a haze
The monsters on my varanda are merely capable to touch me
While you can ruin me.
The goosebumps they rise on my skin
Hearing your hyperbolic talking
And the illicit way you sharpen your knife when I'm sleeping
Can't wipe the smirk off your face.
I'm not afraid of the dark
The monsters are hiding behind the Daisy bushes
I'm fighting off the demon on my bed
One step and it can sabotage me within a second.
Your tansy smile now looks like poison ivy.

21. Haze

Is this the reality or a nightmare?
Am I the murderer or the victim?
I see no colours
Not black and white
It's all blurring together
All I see is a haze.
The moon rises
And the sun sets
Those moments of replay
Screaming and crying
Getting lost in the rain
All I see is a haze.
Now it's too late
But I survived
Dreaming about it each night
Getting lost in my own head
You call it self destruction
I call it grief
All I see is haze.
My dreams have invaded my poetry
On each page of my notebook is a stain of you
I was dazzled by your light

The tears blurred my vision
Now, all I see is haze.
What were you
The murderer or the savior?

22. For my person

Darling ,
I would lean on you
and kiss your lips ,
while holding your hands up
And rubbing the legs against you .
I would kiss you till you're unable to breath .
I would warm you up
and make your body sweat .
I would hold your waist
and kiss the curves of your body .
I would dim the lights around
and uncover the clothes ,
and press the soft cushions of yours .
I would eat your lucious lips
and make them puffier .
I would run my fingers all over your body ,
till it makes you out of breath !
By the end ,
we would be gasping for breath .

23. Paroxysm

It was as if I was drowning
As if the water was filling my lungs
As my head sunk farther and farther in the water
Clouding my vision
I was gasping for breath
But I couldn't breathe
I was taking in deep breaths
I could see where my freedom was
As if it was taunting me.
I felt as I took in the air
And it filled my burning lungs
The world didn't make any sense
I was desperately trying to breathe
But it wasn't enough
My lung was still burning.
Tears were clouding my vision
I was seeing black
A single drop rolled down my eyes
I need a lot more to survive
I didn't have that in me to try any harder
I could see my death approaching
I was glad that atleast this pain would be over

My head was spinning
I was letting myself go
I was drowning to the ocean bed
My voice was getting blocked
No one could hear me screaming.
It was just me fighting the demons in the corner of the school corridor
So much for falling in love with you
Just on seeing you
I wish that my body lied there lifeless
I didn't have it anymore to fight
On seeing you it was as if I couldn't breathe.
Just me and my death throes.

How Is You Heart?

Did the twin flame bruise paint you blue
    Your heart is so addictive
    I pity people who don't know how it feels to be so in love
    All these people think love's for show but I'd die for you in secret
    I'm afraid to let go because you won't even bother to catch me
    I guess we never knew we had the shortest forever
    You'll see the truth somewhere in my eyes.

9 798889 860211

Printed by Libri Plureos GmbH in Hamburg,
Germany